TEACHING BEGINNING

PAT CAMPBELL

- Think Alouds
- LEA
- DRTA
- Cloze
- Phonics
- Word Families
- Sight Words
- K-W-L

Teaching Beginning Readers © 2010 Grass Roots Press

Grass Roots Press
A division of Literacy Services of Canada Ltd.
www.grassrootsbooks.net

Author: Pat Campbell
Editor: Linda Kita-Bradley
Illustrator: Jamie Treat
Design: Lara Minja
Layout: Susan Hunter

Acknowledgements

We acknowledge the support of the Office of Literacy and Essential Skills, Human Resources and Skills Development Canada.

We acknowledge the financial support of the Government of Canada through the Book Publishing Industry Development Program (BPIDP) for our publishing activities.

We acknowledge the support of the Alberta Foundation for the Arts for our publishing programs.

We would also like to acknowledge

Vancouver Community College for granting us permission to adapt their grocery list activity.

The Globe and Mail for granting us permission to reprint an excerpt from "100 years old and a man of letters."

ISBN: 978-1-926583-13-6

Preface

Although beginning readers have a range of understanding and knowledge of the world and of the way things work, they may also be marginalized in many ways. Their struggles with reading can limit access to opportunities in the community and workplace. Their educational choices are restricted because many colleges do not offer upgrading classes to beginning readers. Their choice of reading material is narrow because mainstream educational publishers do not produce adult-oriented books for beginning readers. Yet, according to Statistics Canada, close to one million Canadians have very low-literacy skills.[1]

Organization of the Manual

The introduction examines why one million adults have difficulty reading very simple text such as grocery lists. A *Globe and Mail* article then provides a compelling story about Clarence, a man who learned to read at the age of 93. The next section presents a list of ten principles for teaching beginning readers. This section is followed by responses to three frequently asked questions: (1) Where do I start? (2) Do I need to teach skills in a particular order? and (3) What do I teach? The primary focus of the manual is dedicated to describing instructional activities, many of which are geared towards educators who work in a one-to-one tutoring situation; however, the activities can be modified for classroom instruction. It is recommended that educators begin teaching with language experience stories and sight words, then choose other strategies based on the student's learning needs. The manual concludes with sample lesson plans, a resource list, and glossary.

Acknowledgements

This manual is a companion piece to the assessment kit *Diagnostic Adult Literacy Assessment for Beginning Readers* (DALA). The assessment project was sponsored by the Centre for Education and Work in Winnipeg, Manitoba. I would like to thank Dr. Robin Millar, the Executive Director, and Maria Gill, the Associate Director, for providing the resources and support to undertake and complete this project.

I would also like to thank Avril Lewis, Tina Natale, and Janet Isserlis for their words of encouragement and feedback about this manual. Finally, a big thank you to Terry, my ever-patient husband, who understands the challenges of writing and deadlines, and who is always by my side during the emotional rollercoaster ride that accompanies these challenges. ∎

---

1. According to Statistics Canada, 3.7 percent of the participants in the International Adult Literacy and Skills Survey (IALSS) failed the core test, which consisted of six simple literacy tasks. This alarming statistic indicates that close to one million Canadians would be unable to complete the full IALSS test because of their very low-literacy skills.

Contents

Introduction, 5
Clarence's Story, 7
Principles for Working with Beginning Readers, 12
Putting the Pieces Together, 18

Strategies

CORE
- Language Experience Approach, 22
- Sight Words, 26

COMPREHENSION
- The Cloze Procedure, 28
- Think-Aloud Strategy, 30
- Directed Reading Thinking Activity, 32
- Invisible Messages, 34
- K-W-L, 36

FLUENCY
- Echo Reading, 37
- Repeated Reading, 38

PRINT-SOUND RELATIONSHIPS
- Environmental Print, 40
- Phonemic Awareness, 42
- Phonics, 45
- Word Families, 46

WRITING
- Frame Sentences, 48
- Emergent Writing, 50
- Look, Say, Cover, Print, and Check, 51

Activities
- Photo Album, 52
- Sight Word Bingo, 54
- Photo Story, 55
- Picture Dictionary, 56
- Word Slide, 57

Lesson Planning
- Guidelines for Successful Learning, 58
- Case Studies, 59
- Values and Beliefs, 67

Resources, 68
Glossary, 70
References, 72

Introduction

> When we come back from school, there's nobody there, like to help us with homeworks. Not nothing. I can't remember, like growing up as a kid, like nobody ever take like a storybook and say like read to you as a kid or something. I could never remember that...I never miss a day from going to school. And number one, you go to school, the classroom, they is overcrowded. And when you come back, you have no background. Nobody to help you.
>
> (Carmel, 2003, p. 77)

> My mother tells a story about me when I was three. I was obsessed with books and I desperately wanted to read. One of my favourite books was *The [Tale of] Flopsy Bunnies* by Beatrice Potter. I would make my mom read it to me over and over again until I had memorized it, including when to turn the pages. My party trick was to read the book to people, including the line, 'It made them feel soporific'—it always terrified people to see this three-year-old talking about feeling soporific.
>
> (Ouchi, 2005, p. 57)

Think back to your childhood. How did you learn to read? Quite often, fluent readers do not remember how they learned to read, but with a bit of reflection, they can remember the journey. Some people, unfortunately, did not fully experience the journey. They were left behind.

Some people assume that beginning readers speak English as a second language. While this is sometimes the case, many beginning readers were born in Canada and their first language is English. This begs the question, Given the fact that Canada's publicly funded educational system is compulsory up to the age of 16, why can't some adults read or write a grocery list?

There is no simple answer to this question, but there are some common scenarios. Quite often, the adults' early experiences with written language were limited. If preschoolers are not engaged with specific and varying types of literacy practices, they will be at a considerable disadvantage when they start elementary school. These children might not possess the emergent literacy concepts needed for school success. Sometimes they never reach the literacy levels attained by their peers, and many end up dropping out of school, frustrated and humiliated. As adults, some tend to blame themselves for their inability to read rather than acknowledging systemic factors.

Socio-economic factors also contribute to low literacy. Many learners have limited access to quality education, as many school districts are underfunded and lack resources. During interviews, adult learners would tell me about their transient lives as children. They moved from place to place and school to school, as their parent(s) or guardian(s) looked for work and an affordable place to live. Poverty and health challenges often go hand in hand; many adult learners missed a substantial part of their early schooling due to illness. Others were raised in a home or community where economic survival took precedence over formal learning. Gaps in education and sporadic school attendance, especially when foundational concepts were being taught, impacted these learners' literacy development.

Finally, some adults did not receive the reading instruction they required while in elementary school. While many children learn to read, no matter how they are taught, some do not. Some children require a diagnostic assessment in order to identify their strengths and specific learning needs.

This manual is based on the premise that each beginning reader brings individual strengths, experiences, and knowledge to the learning environment. The *Diagnostic Adult Literacy Assessment for Beginning Readers* (DALA) is a diagnostic tool that, together with the reading strategies outlined in this manual, can be used as a basis of instruction that meets the specific learning needs of beginning readers. ■

Clarence's Story

In 2006, the *Globe and Mail* featured the following story about Clarence, a man who taught himself to read at the age of 93. At the age of 103, Clarence is still reading and still going for his daily walks.

Before you read Clarence's story, make a list of your assumptions about adults who are beginning readers. As you read Clarence's story, think about these questions:

- As a child, what barriers prevented Clarence from learning to read?
- Why did Clarence learn to read?
- How did Clarence learn to read?

When 100-year-old Clarence Brazier decided, at 93, that he'd have to learn to read his junk mail if he ever hoped to shop for himself, it was a matter of necessity — just as taking over the family farm had been when he was barely old enough to tie his shoes let alone shoe a horse.

He had spent most of his life in Timmins, Ont., where he and his wife Angela had retired to their own farm. They were married 64 years, but when she died after a long illness, he suddenly had no one to keep his great secret any longer.

His beloved "Angel" had always taken care of the written words. Clarence was the family talker — "I could bullshit," he laughs — and he had even been head of a local political constituency and farmers' union while she had served as secretary, faithfully covering his tracks. No one but the immediate family, Angela and their four daughters, ever knew the truth.

Teaching Beginning Readers 7

Seven years ago, however, there was no longer an Angel to watch over him. He had to eat, but he didn't even know how to shop. He took knife and scissors and cut labels off boxes in the pantry and went down to the store and tried to match colours and symbols, but that proved only frustrating and embarrassing to him.

"I had used tricks my whole life to get by," he says. But now the tricks were failing him.

The only solution, he finally concluded, was to learn the words.

"I started with the junk mail they delivered to my house," he says. The mail would come and he would spend hours out on the stoop of the farmhouse trying to pronounce words he knew were on the flyers. He knew the Canadian Tire symbol and tried to work through the letters to see how the word formed. He knew "pizza" and "hamburger" and "fries" from the pictures and memorized those letters. Rug cleaning, snow plowing, real-estate listings, grocery specials. . . .

"It is difficult for me to stress how hard and tedious and frustrating those hours were," he says.

Knowing her father was now alone, his daughter Doris Villemaire, a retired school teacher, asked if he would like to come down south and move in with her and her husband, Jim Villemaire. Clarence agreed, even though he was still perfectly capable of caring for himself, the shopping excepted.

Doris couldn't help noticing how her father was picking through the newspaper for the flyers. He would trace over words now familiar, still trying to figure out how all the words in the newspaper made sense. After years working in mines and running chainsaws without ear protection, his hearing was rapidly deteriorating to the point where he wasn't watching television and listening to the radio the way he used to. Clarence had always been a man who kept up with politics and world affairs, but now the only way he could get at that information, he figured, was if he learned to read that newspaper he'd spent a lifetime avoiding.

Doris asked her father if he would like help. She was volunteering for the Muskoka Literacy Council and had access to material. She brought him home some primary readers, Grade 1 level, and together they worked through the alphabet and words so simple he laughs now to recall them.

"C-A-T, cat! R-A-T, rat! They were not very interesting." He had higher ambitions. He wanted to read the newspaper to find out what was going on today. He wanted to read books to find out what had gone on in the North Country in his day.

And he wanted to get the education he had never had. He didn't think he was stupid. He just had no schooling.

"I had a lot of education, actually," he says.

"But, you know, I stole it."

Clarence was five years old when his life turned upside down.

His father, George Brazier, was using explosives one day to blow out a stump, and when the charge failed he went to inspect the fuse. It exploded as he knelt over the stump, blowing his right eyeball out and blinding the left eye.

Fanny Mae Brazier was left with a husband who could not see a thing, six children and the mortgage. Little Clarence was third-oldest but also, by far, the most capable one when it came to taking care of the cattle and horses. Within two years, by age seven, he was running the farm operation on his own.

In the winter months, the children did go to school, but Clarence — sprouting fast to his eventual six-foot-two — was both tallest in his class and furthest behind. He was humiliated by appearing so dull and being ridiculed. He never even finished Grade 1.

He was imaginative. Farmers disliked the way blood would spray over the snow during the de-horning and Clarence devised a system using old socks to stem the flow so the cutting could be done in the barn, with the blood flowing down into gutters where it could be washed away.

"It was a simple thing to think of," he says.

Clarence was also inventive and a quick learner, but he felt totally inadequate in that he had no education whatsoever and could not even read a sign. "It was always on my mind," he says. "I knew if I didn't read that I had better learn to do something else to replace it."

Clarence worked in the Timmins gold mines, the Sudbury nickel mines, as a travelling brush salesman and as a security guard. "I had schemes in every place I worked," he says. He tried to befriend someone who could read who might cover for him.

As soon as a promotion would come along that might involve paperwork, he quit. He had dozens of jobs, quit dozens of jobs, yet was never short of work. His shortest job lasted one day — almost. He had been doing security work in Timmins and landed a job as a guard at the infamous Don Jail in Toronto. He moved down, showed up for work and was told that, at the end of his shift, he'd have to fill in a report. He quit on the spot.

When Clarence was well into his 20s, a new family, the Boudreaus, moved in from New Brunswick. They had a young daughter, Angela, who was quickly noticed. Angela was very bright. She would later earn a college diploma, but at this point she had already dropped out of school in Grade 6.

The Boudreaus spoke French and there was only an English school for her to attend, so she quit in frustration.

"She was very, very smart for the education she had," Clarence says. "She was up to mark on everything."

Angela was behind him when he worked for the local New Democratic Party; she helped him when he headed up the farmers' union. She handled the bills, the applications, everything that involved paperwork.

Together they raised their four daughters, all pushed to get higher education, all successful in their own careers. And all moved away, leaving Clarence and Angela in Timmins to grow old together.

But then, one day, Clarence no longer had his crutch.

"I learned to read," he says, "all because I lost my wife."

"He was a very enthusiastic student."

Doris remembers those first months with the primary readers.

"His eyes would actually sparkle when he'd recognize a word. It was just as I'd seen with my students, but it was also kind of funny, too. I was seeing this same thing in my father — and he was acting just like the children I'd taught."

From junk mail he moved to primary readers, and from primary readers to children's books and then into youth novels.

From fiction he headed into non-fiction, and today sits surrounded by books on history, books on mining and logging, books on Northern Ontario and hockey and Canada. The newspaper is at his feet, the various sections dropped as he has read through them.

He reads at least two hours a day. Often, at night, he will wake and read himself back to sleep.

His life has changed dramatically. No longer hiding his inability to read, he now brags about it. He goes to the area seniors' homes — "visiting with the young lads," he says — and tells those who are well into their 60s and 70s and do not bother with books that "They've got 30 years of good reading ahead of them."

"I can't hear the television or listen to the radio to keep current with events and politics," says.

"Had I not learned to read, I believe I would have slowly become isolated from the world beyond my home."

Instead, as Clarence moves into his second century, that world is opening up.

In the fall of 2006 Canada Post presented him with the National Literacy Award.

At age 100, he has just become the poster boy for the very thing he spent nearly a century avoiding.

> Begin challenging your own assumptions. Your assumptions are your windows on the world. Scrub them off every once in awhile, or the light won't come through.
> –Alan Alda

Did the article about Clarence's story challenge your assumptions about beginning readers? In what ways does the article support or challenge your knowledge of and beliefs about adults learning to read? The most important lesson that I have learned as a literacy educator is to question my assumptions. Before we can challenge our assumptions, we need to heighten our awareness of them. This is easier said than done because we often fail to view assumptions as assumptions. Instead, we view assumptions as facts or truth or common sense. We need to reflect carefully on the assumptions underlying our teaching practice. If we can identify and test our assumptions to make sure they are based in reality, we will improve our practice.

Principles for Working with Beginning Readers

The following principles are based on research from the field of emergent and adult literacy research.

1. The instructional program incorporates a balanced approach.

A balanced literacy program integrates reading *and* writing instruction. Students are encouraged to engage in literacy activities that are connected to their daily lives. For example, writing activities should focus on a specific purpose, such as creating a grocery list or signing a birthday card. Reading instruction should include reading and discussing authentic text that students encounter outside the classroom.

A balanced program places equal emphasis on print and meaning-centred literacy activities. Print-centred activities, such as teaching phonics and *the alphabetic principle*, draw the students' attention to letters and sounds. Meaning-centred activities stress the importance of producing meaning (rather than word-perfect reading), which encourages students to take risks.

Alphabetic Principle: the understanding that letters in written words stand for sounds in spoken words.

2. The primary purpose of assessment is to inform instruction.

Assessment for learning is a participatory process in which students actively engage in assessment tasks and dialogue, which leads to a deeper understanding of how they learn and what they know. Through this understanding, the assessment will achieve its primary purpose, which is to inform learning and teaching.

The intake literacy assessment provides essential diagnostic information that enables you to design individualized lesson plans, choose relevant materials, and implement effective teaching strategies. The intake interview, which is at the heart of the assessment, entails gathering information about students' goals, literacy practices, and interests. Some literacy educators question the point of assessing an adult who "can't" read. Yet, even adults who view themselves as "non-readers" possess literacy knowledge and skills. For instance, many beginning readers can read some environmental print and can recognize letter names. Insightful, diagnostic assessment provides opportunities for students to demonstrate what they can do rather than what they cannot do.

Formative assessment needs to be an integral and ongoing part of teaching and learning. Tracking student progress allows you to adjust your instruction to better meet the student's ever-changing learning needs.

> "Formative assessment refers to frequent, interactive assessments of student progress and understanding" (OECD, p. 16).

3. The instructional program responds to the student's learning needs.

Each beginning reader is at a different point on the continuum of literacy development. Students who are *acquiring* a specific skill will be at a different point along the learning continuum from those who are *building* their ability with a specific skill. Consequently, instruction needs to be tailored to a student's level of competence for a particular skill.

For example, phonics instruction that is based on the student's knowledge is more effective than teaching phonics in a predetermined sequence. Beginning readers usually possess some phonics knowledge. For instance, if a student's name is Tyrone, he might know that the letter "t" makes the /t/ sound. Once you have determined the student's needs, integrate the phonics instruction into your lessons.

As educators, we need to be wary of commercial programs such as *Hooked on Phonics*, because the one-size-fits-all approach will not meet the individual learning needs of beginning readers. Such programs may provide useful ideas but inevitably require modification and adaptation.

4. Students are actively involved in the learning process.

Research shows that students learn best when they are actively engaged in the learning process. In an active learning environment, students define their goals and participate in choosing materials and activities, making decisions, and evaluating their progress. Students who feel responsible for their learning are more apt to transfer and apply their literacy skills into the home and community. Some students are eager to take ownership of their learning while others are reluctant. Students who come from a culture that views the teacher as the expert might feel uncomfortable about taking control of their learning. Likewise, a student's reluctance may stem from past experiences when they were excluded from participating in decision making, as often happens in the working-class sector. It is important for educators to relinquish control so that students do not adopt a passive role in their learning.

5. Instruction includes discussion about the student's conceptual understanding of reading.

Students may have restricted notions about what it means to be a reader and how one learns to read. Misconceptions about reading might hinder ability to learn, so it becomes important for educators and students to share views and discuss differences of opinion regarding the reading process. By providing opportunities for group discussion, students will gain a deeper and clearer understanding of what it means to be a reader.

An excellent starting point is the question, Why do people read? A beginning reader may approach all text in the same way, whether attempting to read a discount coupon or a report card. Through discussion, students learn that one's approach to text depends on their purpose for reading it.

Responses to the question, What does it mean to be a good reader? can provide valuable information about why students prefer certain reading strategies over others. For instance, if adults were exposed to phonics instruction during their primary education, they may believe that good readers sound out every letter or that "guessing" unfamiliar words is a form of cheating. In this case, educators can broaden and deepen these students' concept of reading by discussing how good readers use their background knowledge to decode and interpret text. By asking questions such as, What do you do when you come across a word you don't know?, and What do you do if you don't understand something you have read?, educators gain further insight into the students' awareness and knowledge of reading strategies.

Beginning readers engage in a range of literacy activities that support their everyday life functions and interests. Yet, students might say "I don't read anything" because, to them, reading means picking up a book or newspaper. Therefore, it is important to validate all of their everyday reading activities. Beginning readers need to recognize

> A beginning reader may approach all text in the same way, whether attempting to read a discount coupon or a report card.

that, for example, looking at a sign such as Exit or Open and understanding the meaning behind the word constitutes reading. By asking, What food labels did you read in your home today? or What signs did you read on your way to class?, students will begin to view themselves as readers.

6. Students and educators discuss their expectations.

Students often have expectations about how they will be taught and the time it will take for them to become fluent readers. Students and educators need opportunities to voice their expectations so that they can come to a common understanding. If discussion does not occur, students and educators may experience frustration or anger because expectations are not being met. For example, beginning readers might not realize that in order to make the transition from being beginning readers to fluent readers, they need to apply and transfer the skills they have learned within the classroom to their everyday life. Students who restrict their reading to that which occurs within the four walls of the classroom might become frustrated with their lack of progress. They might leave the program rather than express their dissatisfaction. Without fully understanding the situation, the educator might label these students as unmotivated.

7. Instruction builds upon and validates student's experiences and knowledge.

Adult literacy learning is most successful when students are encouraged to express their ideas and opinions and draw on their interests and experiences. Knowing student's interests will help you choose topics for language experience stories. Knowing how they use literacy in their daily lives will guide the choice of literacy materials that will be used during instruction.

Several instructional techniques and materials serve to elicit and utilize students' background knowledge and experiences. When students read language experience stories, they can use their background knowledge and meaning cues to predict unfamiliar words. Comprehension activities such as Directed Reading Thinking Activity (DRTA) and K-W-L encourage students to activate their background knowledge and relate it to stories that the educator reads out loud.

DRTA and K-W-L are featured on pages 32 and 35.

8. Instruction supports the two cueing systems: print and meaning.

Many people think that phonics instruction is the key to learning how to read. However, research shows that beginning readers use different reading strategies to decode unfamiliar words (Campbell & Malicky, 2002). The degree of reliance on print-based and meaning-based cues and the ability to integrate these two sources of information varies from student to student. For example, students who try to sound out each and every letter in a word are relying too heavily on print cues. This type of reader will benefit from instruction in the cloze procedure, which places a heavier focus on meaning. Likewise, students who rely too heavily on meaning cues to predict unfamiliar words will benefit from phonics instruction.

9. Reading material is authentic.

Authentic text is material that adults encounter in everyday life, such as novels, newspapers, recipes, emails, bank statements, bills, instructions, and memos. The authentic material that can be read by beginning readers is restricted because of the difficulty of the text. For beginning readers, authentic text includes language experience stories, photostories, and environmental print such as flyers, coupons, signs, food labels, and calendars. Using relevant and authentic resources, rather than relying on worksheets with little or no connection to the students' lives, makes for much more meaningful lessons.

Phonics instruction, for example, needs to be embedded in authentic, meaningful activities. If the student can read the word *Monday* on a calendar, the relationship between "m" and /m/ can be introduced. Using the sight word "Monday" to introduce a new letter and sound enhances learning by moving from the familiar to the unfamiliar, from the concrete to the abstract, and from the whole to the part.

10. Opportunities are provided for learning circles.

Studies have shown that students value a sense of community in their literacy programs.

This strong desire for community points to the need to balance the "each one teach one" model of instruction with small group instruction. The primary way in which students can begin to see that personal problems are social issues is through talking with one another. While the learning centre may or may not be a place where students engage in advocacy, as such, it can certainly provide adults with access to one another's ideas and opinions on topics ranging from dealing with stress to child rearing to finding a good doctor. These conversations can be the springboard for dialogue and a contextualized literacy education that recognizes the collective, social purpose of education rather than a decontextualized, depoliticized functional education that stresses only the skill needs of the individual student.

Putting the Pieces Together

This section addresses three questions that are frequently posed by literacy educators who work with beginning readers.

Where do I start?

I need to practice spelling numbers so I can write cheques.

Through initial and ongoing discussion, you can find out the answer to a key question, what does the student want to learn? The student's response to this question is your starting point. Sometimes students will generalize and say, "I want to learn to read or write." As students learn more about what it is they can do with print, their ideas about what they want to learn will expand accordingly. By knowing what the student wants, you can design student-centred lessons that incorporate authentic materials and activities. Lessons will gradually build on one another as you and the student continue to work together.

The first meeting is an opportunity to learn about the role of literacy in the student's daily life. You can find out how the student uses or needs to use literacy at home, in the community, and at work. Many beginning readers enrol in a literacy program because of an immediate need. For example, a student might have been hired as a short-order cook and needs to read the servers' orders. In this scenario, you would begin by developing the student's repertoire of sight words for food. If the student is working in a restaurant where servers take orders by hand, you might also practise reading different sorts of handwriting—printing, cursive, all caps, etc.

During your first set of lessons, focus on the student's strengths. Adults can read and make sense of their world. They recognize and interpret symbols, make inferences, draw conclusions, and analyze and synthesize information. They possess a high degree of knowledge based on past experiences and an extensive vocabulary. Adults bring their knowledge of the world to the learning context. They rely on meaning cues or a combination of meaning and print cues to decode words. Read the language experience story on the next page:

My brother and I go ice fishing.
The ice can be real thick. We cut a hole with the auger.
We drop our jigs down the hole.
Sometimes, it real slow.
You have to be patient.

Let's say you and the student have read the story together several times, and the student is ready to read it independently. However, she falters on the words "auger" and "patient." Rather than asking her to sound out these words, which would be extremely difficult, emphasize the use of meaning cues. You might ask, what word would make sense? By asking this question, you are requiring the student to use her background knowledge and meaning cues to predict the word.

Lessons that emphasize and reinforce the use of background knowledge to identify words and construct meaning are a good starting point for beginning readers. This is because you are focusing on the students' strengths—what they already know—rather than on what they do not know. This does not mean that strategies for processing print should be neglected. However, the first set of lessons should focus on meaning-based strategies. You can then gradually ease into using print to decode words.

Do I need to teach skills in a particular order?

Some educators believe that individuals learn to read by progressing through a linear, sequential series of skills. It is assumed that learning to read is easier if adults master one skill at a time, beginning with the smallest unit of analysis (E.g., letters and sounds) and gradually moving to larger units such as words. In fact, many publishers produce workbooks that are based on this assumption. In such texts, Lesson 1 introduces students to the consonant "b," and they perform drill exercises for reinforcement. Once students have mastered the consonants, they move onto a new workbook that introduces them to the vowel sounds. However, this type of approach is based on a deficit perspective; the instructional focus is on the students' weaknesses—the skills they do not possess—rather than on their strengths, their knowledge, and the reading skills they do possess.

Beginning readers will benefit by instruction that provides them with familiar and meaningful text that is highly predictable and easy to read.

Language experience stories and sight words are core instructional strategies. Once the student has experienced success with reading a language experience story and sight words, you can incorporate a balanced set of strategies that develop fluency, comprehension, knowledge of speech and print relationships, and writing. (See illustration below.)

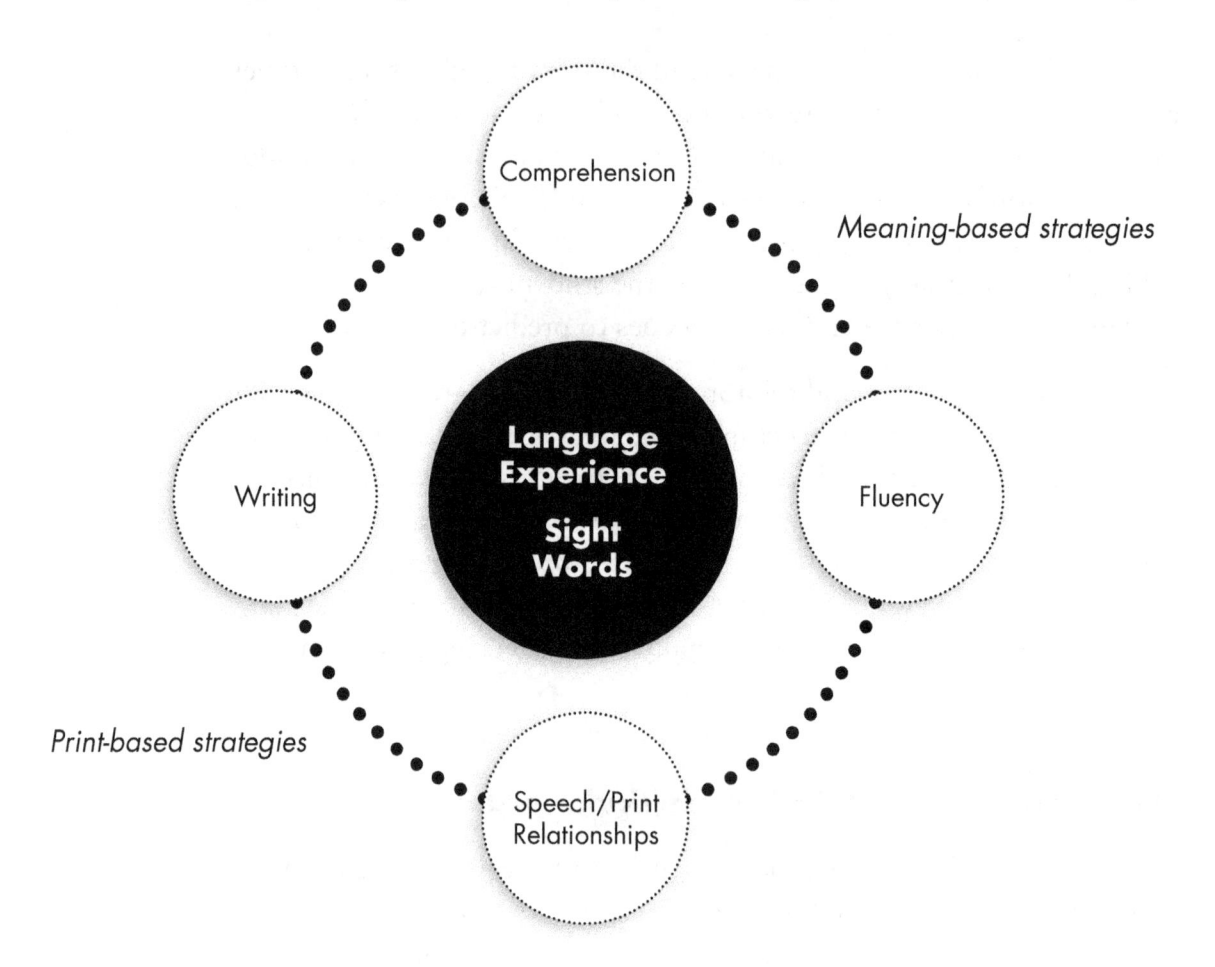

```
                    Comprehension

                                        Meaning-based strategies

    Writing      Language Experience      Fluency
                    Sight Words

Print-based strategies

                  Speech/Print
                  Relationships
```

What do I need to teach?

The *Diagnostic Adult Reading Assessment for Beginning Readers* assesses the student's skills. The student's performance can guide your instruction. You can find out whether the student knows print concepts such as the meaning of the terms "sentence," "letter," "period," and "question mark." If the student is unfamiliar with these terms, you can teach them. Or, you might find that the student's phonemic awareness is well-developed, but they need some phonics instruction. The assessment will pinpoint the consonant and vowel sounds the student needs to learn.

The chart on the next page links assessment to instruction by showing the instructional implications for the DALA subtests.

DALA SUBTESTS	A strong performance indicates the student	A weak performance suggests the student needs
ENVIRONMENTAL PRINT	is aware of and attuned to environmental print.	to interact with print in meaningful ways. (See pages 40 to 41.)
TEXT FUNCTIONS	understands the uses and purposes of text.	to be exposed to a variety of authentic texts and discuss their uses and purposes.
PRINT CONCEPTS AND CONVENTIONS	has a conceptual understanding of print features and conventions.	instruction in specific print concepts and terms such as "word" and "letter", etc.
LETTER NAMES	can distinguish between the symbols of the alphabet.	to learn specific upper or lower case letter names.
PHONEMIC AWARENESS: BEGINNING SOUNDS	can isolate initial phonemes in spoken words.	instruction in phonemic awareness. (See pages 42 to 43.)
PHONEMIC AWARENESS: RHYMES	can recognize oral rhymes.	instruction in phonemic awareness and word families. (See pages 42, 43 and 46.)
HIGH FREQUENCY WORDS	has stored a repertoire of sight words in his/her visual memory.	to instantly recognize high-frequency words. (See pages 25 to 26.)
PHONICS KNOWLEDGE	understands letter-sound relationships.	to learn specific sound-letter relationships. (See pages 44 to 45.)
ALPHABETIC PRINCIPLE	understands that letters in written words stand for sounds in spoken words.	to develop knowledge of the alphabetic principle. (See page 50.)
LITERACY PRACTICES	N/A	N/A

CORE

Language Experience Approach

PURPOSES:

To provide familiar, meaningful text that is predictable and easy to read.

To establish the link between spoken and written words.

STEPS:

1. Invite the student to share a personal experience or provide the student with a prompt. (See the list of prompts on the next page.)

2. Encourage the student to tell a story about the experience or prompt.

3. Record the story, making sure the student can see the words being printed. Record the student's exact words, printing clearly on every second line. Say each word as you print it.

4. Read the story, pointing to each word as you read. Ask the student if they want to make any changes.

5. Read the story together several times, tracking the words with your finger. Ask the student to read the story independently. If the student falters, provide support by reading the word.

Notes:

Initially, record three or four sentences from the story. As the student gains skills and confidence, you can record longer stories.

Type up the story for future use. Print out and store the story in a folder or binder.

22 Core Strategies

Language Experience Prompts

These prompts can be used over time. As learners become familiar with the language experience process, they might be invited to suggest prompts as well.

- Tell me about: your first job.
                       a gift you made for someone.
                       your favourite movie or TV show.
                       one of your dreams.

- Tell me about the last time you: helped someone.
                                    lost something important.
                                    learned something new.
                                    found a great bargain.
                                    cooked a really special meal.

- What would you do if you won the lottery?

- Name five things you are grateful for each day, and why.

- Describe something you have made with your hands.

- If you got a tattoo, where would you put it, what would it be, and why?

- If you could live anywhere in the world, where would it be? Why?

- Describe the best bargain you've ever found at a garage sale.

- If you could be any age again for one week, what age and why?

- If you could have dinner with anyone in the world, who would your dinner guest be, and why?

- If the student has a cellphone with a built-in camera, ask them if they would like to talk about one of their photos.

- Ask the student to choose a photo from a magazine or newspaper and to describe what is happening in the photo.

- Read a letter from an advice column. Ask the student to respond to the letter.

- Read a newspaper article that describes an important issue. Ask the student to express their thoughts on the issue.

Sample Language Experience Story

My Usual Day

I get up at four o'clock in the morning and I make myself some tea. I get a shower and then put on my clothes to go to my work. I take the bus at a quarter to five in the early morning and I get to the subway at five. I have to take a next (bus) and then another one that takes me to another place. From there, I still have to take another bus or I can walk to the place. If it's a nice day, I walk there. At (work), I pick orders for a big (food) store. I work in the freezer section. This is a new job for me. I been there for four months now and I had to pass a test to get in. I like the people there. Them, well they are really nice to me. Now it's only a part-time job, (but) I hope it to be full-time one day. The pay and the (benefits) well, they will be good for me.

Source: From a student enrolled in the Toronto Public Library's Downsview Adult Literacy Program.

The circled words are the student's sight words. The underlined words are the highly predictable words that the educator deleted for a cloze activity. (See page 28.)

24 Core Strategies

Language Experience Activities

SIGHT WORDS

Ask the student to circle five words they would like to learn. Ask them to copy each word on a separate flash card. Ask the student to illustrate the word on the back of the card. The student can then use the illustration as a reminder for the word, when necessary. (Note: Some words such as "and," or "tax" are hard to illustrate.)

CLOZE ACTIVITY

Cover highly predictable words with a small piece of paper. Read the text back to the student. Stop when you reach a covered word and ask the student to predict a word that makes sense and sounds right. Check their predictions by looking at the print.

PHONICS

Select one of the student's sight words (E.g., bus). Say, "Bus starts with the letter 'b.' The sound /b/ goes with the letter 'b.' Can you find some other words in the story that start with the letter 'b'?"

COPYING

Ask the student to copy the language experience story. Writing provides practice in both printing *and* in learning the sound symbol correspondences.

FRAME SENTENCES

Choose a sentence from the language experience story. Write out the first part of the sentence and ask the student to complete the sentence with one word. Write down the word. Repeat the sentence frame, recording all of the student's words.

I make myself some _____.
I make myself some tea.
I make myself some toast.
I make myself some soup.
I make myself some spaghetti.

Sight Words

PURPOSE:

To develop a repertoire of words that can be instantly recognized.

STEPS:

1. Print five words the student wants to learn.

2. Ask the student to copy each word on an index card.

3. Ask the student to close their eyes and make a mental picture of the word. Have the student print the letters of the word in the air, eyes still closed.

4. The student illustrates the word on the back of the index card. Using an illustration enables the student to study the words independently. If the student has difficulty reading the word, they can flip over the card and use the illustration as a reminder. The index cards can be stored, using dividers to separate known words from study words.

> Sight words can include personal words, high-frequency words, and environmental print.

26 Core Strategies

High Frequency Words

The Top 100

a
and
he
I
in
is
it
of
that
the
to
was

These 12 words account for 1/4 of all the words we read every day.

all
are
as
at
be
but
for
had
have
him
his
not
on
one
said
so
they
we
with
you

These 32 words account for 1/3 of all the words we read every day.

about	into	right
an	just	see
back	like	she
been	little	some
before	look	their
big	made	them
by	make	then
call	me	there
came	more	this
can	much	two
come	must	up
could	my	want
did	new	well
do	no	went
down	now	were
first	off	what
from	old	when
get	only	where
go	or	which
has	other	who
her	our	will
here	out	your
if	over	

These 100 words account for 1/2 of all the words we read every day.

Source: www.ladybird.com.

Teaching Beginning Readers 27

COMPREHENSION

The Cloze Procedure

PURPOSE:

To use background knowledge and text information to predict unfamiliar words.

STEPS:

1. Photocopy a passage such as the student's language experience story or a photostory.

2. Leave the first sentence intact to provide context. Delete some of the predictable words with correction fluid or tape. (See example on next page.)

3. Demonstrate the procedure and explain that the student can use information from the sentence to figure out what the word might be. Explain that the word the student chooses needs to make sense and sound right in the sentence.

4. Read the passage out loud to the student, stopping at the deleted words. Ask the student to predict the missing words. If the student cannot predict a word, continue reading to the end of the sentence. Ask the student to try again. Discuss how and why the student selected their words. If the student chooses an inappropriate word, ask, "Why did you choose this word? Does it make sense?" and/or "Does it sound right?"

28 Comprehension Strategies

Sample Cloze Passage

Mandy's Garage Sale

Mandy needs to pay her bills. She needs to _____ some money. She decides to _____ a garage sale. Mandy looks for _____ to sell. She finds some old dishes. Mandy looks for _____ things to sell. She finds some toys. She finds lots of old books. They go into the pile. She looks for more things to sell. She finds an old coat. It is _____ small. It goes into the pile. Then Mandy finds an old camera. It cost a lot. But, the flash does not _____. It goes into the pile. Mandy sets a date for the sale. It will be on June 21. She puts an _____ in the paper. She puts up signs. She puts a price _____ on each item. She puts the things on a table. She _____ out her change. Then she waits. The _____ start to come. A man _____ up the camera. "Wow!" he says. "This is a great camera." Mandy smiles. "Yes," she says, "It is." The man _____ out his money. "Does it work okay?" he asks. Mandy bites her lip. She really needs the money.

Source: Rogers, S. (2003). *Mandy's garage sale.* Edmonton, AB: Grass Roots Press.

Teaching Beginning Readers 29

Think-Aloud Strategy

PURPOSES:

To model how fluent readers engage with text.

To heighten awareness of the strategies fluent readers use to comprehend text.

STEPS:

1. Select a short piece of text that the student will find interesting, such as an article from a newspaper or magazine. Try to find an article that contains a contradiction, some ambiguity, or difficult vocabulary.

2. Read the text out loud. As you read, verbalize what you are thinking.

3. Choose another passage and read it to the student. Stop reading when you come across a piece of text that allows you to describe a visual image, make an inference, a prediction, or a link with prior knowledge. Make a think-aloud and then invite the student to make a think-aloud.

Note:

Stories from local newspapers can work well as the student often will have an opinion or direct experience of the content.

TEXT	THINK-ALOUD	COMMENT
Just as a cougar lunged toward Austin Forman, his guardian Angel stepped in to save the day.	Who is the angel? Is the angel a person?	The reader asks a question and makes a prediction.
The 11-year-old was collecting firewood at his family's home in Boston Bar when his white golden retriever, Angel, thwarted a cougar attack on the youngster.	What does "thwarted" mean? Perhaps as I read on, it will become clear.	The reader identifies an unfamiliar word.
With the dog and cougar locked in a bloody battle, Austin ran into the house screaming for help. "You could hear her whimpering and whining, something you don't ever want to hear again from a dog," said Austin.	One time, I saw my dog get attacked by another dog. It was awful to watch.	The reader makes a link with prior knowledge.
His mom, Sherry, called police, who arrived within minutes and shot the cougar, which had dragged Angel under a set of stairs.	I can just picture the police officer pulling out his revolver and trying to take aim so he wouldn't hit the dog. It was probably dark under the stairs.	The reader describes a visual image and makes an inference.

Source: Adapted from Dormer, D. (2010, January 4). *Dog fends off cougar attack.* The Edmonton Sun.

Directed Reading Thinking Activity (DRTA)

PURPOSES:

To establish a purpose for reading.

To elicit student's prior knowledge.

To encourage the student to monitor comprehension while reading.

STEPS:

1. Select a short fiction or non-fiction passage that provides opportunities to make predictions. Prior to the lesson, predetermine stopping points in the text that lend themselves to making predictions. Prepare the prediction questions you will ask.

2. Show the student any accompanying photos or illustrations and/or read the title. Have the student tell you what they know about the topic. Ask, "What do you think this passage will be about?" Encourage the student to make an initial prediction about content.

3. Read the story out loud to the first selected stopping point. Have the student confirm, refine, or reject their initial prediction. Ask an appropriate question that requires the student to make another prediction.

4. Continue to read the story after the student has made a prediction. Discuss text information that confirms or disproves the student's prediction.

5. Repeat the process of predicting, reading, and evaluating the predictions to the end of the passage.

Sample Passage with Three Stopping Points

Tony's Deal

My name is Tony. My wife Alma and I have two girls. We live in a small house. There is no room for the girls to play. We want to move to a bigger house. We want a house with a yard.

I'm a plumber. I work for myself. I like being my own boss. But, I don't like the paperwork. Sometimes it piles up. I have an ad in the paper. I get lots of calls. This morning I got a call from a guy. ✓

Prediction Question: What do you think the guy wanted?

I went to see the job. Paul wants a bathroom. It's a big job. I tell Paul how much it will cost. "That's too much," says Paul. "Let's do a deal. ✓ How much is it if I pay cash? I don't need a bill." I think, why not? Who needs all that paperwork anyway? So we agree on a price. We shake hands. I'm happy. He's happy.

Prediction Question: What kind of deal do they make?

When I get home, I tell Alma about the deal. ✓ She is not happy. She worries the taxman will find out. "Don't worry," I tell her. "It's just between Paul and me. We can save the money for a bigger house. Besides, everyone makes deals. So how wrong can it be?"

Prediction Question: How do you think Alma will feel? Why?

Source: Kovats, M. (2003). *Tony's deal.* Edmonton, AB: Grass Roots Press.

Invisible Messages

PURPOSE:

To show the student how to use background knowledge and text cues to make inferences.

STEPS:

❶ Explain the importance of inferences. Say, "Writers do not always tell the reader everything. Sometimes writers expect readers to figure out the missing information. Readers make an inference when they try to figure out the writer's invisible message."

❷ Read a short portion of text and make an inference. Explain how you were able to make the inference.

❸ Read another short portion of text and ask the student to make an inference. Ask the student to explain how they made the inference.

> **Biographies and newspaper articles featuring people are a good source of text for making inferences. Students can make inferences about a person's character by reading about their actions.**

34 Comprehension Strategies

Sample Invisible Messages

TEXT	INVISIBLE MESSAGE (INFERENCE)
Mother Teresa lives in a convent. On Sundays, she visits the poor. She visits hungry people. She visits sick people. She visits dying people. These people are the "poorest of the poor."	Mother Teresa is a nun.
Mother Teresa opens a school in the slums. The school has no walls. The school has no books. The school has no blackboards. Mother Teresa uses a stick to write letters in the mud. The poor children learn to read and write.	Mother Teresa believes that everybody has the right to learn.
Mother Teresa sees people die on the streets. They need to see doctors. They need medicine. But they have no money. Mother Teresa wants to care for the poor and sick. She wants to learn basic medicine.	There is no free health care system for the poor.

Source: Barber, T. (2006). *Mother Teresa.* Edmonton, AB: Grass Roots Press.

K-W-L

PURPOSES:

To promote active reading.

To activate background knowledge and set a purpose for reading.

STEPS:

1. Select a non-fiction passage on a topic that reflects the student's interests or needs (E.g., Alzheimer's disease).

2. Ask the student what they know about the topic.

3. Ask the student what they would like to learn about the topic. Record the questions.

    E.g., My dad has it. Will I get it?

    Is there a cure?

    Are there any drugs to treat Alzheimer's disease?

4. Read the passage. Then discuss what the student learned about the topic. Check to see if the student's questions were answered. If the student's questions were not answered, discuss possible ways to find the answers.

Note:

The acronym K-W-L stands for:
- what I know.
- what I want to know.
- what I learned.

FLUENCY

Echo Reading

PURPOSES:

To improve reading fluency.

To gain exposure to a variety of text.

STEPS:

1. Choose a simple, familiar piece of text, such as a language experience story or a photostory, that is at the student's instructional level.

2. Read the first sentence to the student. Move your finger along the line of print, matching the speed and flow of the oral reading. Place your finger directly under each word as it is read.

3. Ask the student to read the sentence independently. Do not correct any mistakes the student may make. (If the student falters, read the sentence together.)

Notes:

After the student gains confidence:
- use simple, *unfamiliar* pieces of text.
- increase the number of sentences that are read at one time.
- have the student point to each word as they read it.

Repeated Reading

PURPOSES:

To improve fluency.

To experience success in reading continuous text.

STEPS:

1. Select a language experience story.

2. Have the student read a 50- to 100-word selection from the story. Explain that you want the student to read the selection several times over the next five weeks because reading improves with practice. Explain that you will time how long it takes them to read the passage in order to show progress.

3. The student reads the story orally and independently. If the student falters, provide support by reading the word. Time each reading and record the time in a chart.

4. Engage the student in discussion about the story. Practise the difficult words.

5. At the next lesson, have the student read the story again. Time the reading and record the time on the chart to show progress.

Note:

As the student gains confidence, you can provide more difficult and longer reading material.

Sample: Repeated Reading Chart

Number of Times I Read the Story/Passage

Reading Time (Minutes:Seconds)	1	2	3	4	5
2:00					
2:30					
3:00					X
3:30				X	
4:00					
4:30			X		
5:00					
5:30		X			
6:00	X				

Teaching Beginning Readers 39

PRINT-SOUND RELATIONSHIPS

Environmental Print: Walk About

PURPOSES:

To increase the student's repertoire of sight words that they can recognize in the community.

To pay attention to the letters and sounds in environmental print and to transfer this knowledge to decontextualized print.

STEPS:

1. Walk around the student's community. If it is impractical to walk around the community, consider meeting the student at a convenient place such as a grocery store to photograph environmental print. Identify all the environmental print (E.g., Open, Push, For Rent, Post Office, Bowman Street, Subway). Have the student indicate which words they can and cannot read. Have the student take photos of the words they want to learn to read. (Bring a digital camera with you.)

2. Print out the photos.

3. At the next lesson, discuss the words in the photos. Ask questions that draw the student's attention to the letters and sounds in the words:
   - What letter do you see at the beginning of this word?
   - What sound does the letter make?
   - Are there any other words that begin with this letter?

4. Add the photos to the student's picture dictionary.

(See page 56.)

40 Print-Sound Relationship Strategies

Environmental Print: Brand Names

PURPOSES:

To pay attention to the letters and sounds in brand names and to transfer this knowledge to decontextualized print.

STEPS:

1. Show the student some examples of brand names. With the student's help, collect boxes, packages, bottles, plastic food containers, and cans that contain brand names (E.g., Kelloggs, Coca-Cola, M&M's).

2. Print out each brand name on an index card.

3. Review the brand names. Ask the student to match the brand names on the boxes, packages, etc. to the print on the index card.

4. Ask questions that draw that student's attention to the letters and sounds in the brand names:
   - What letter do you see at the beginning of this brand name?
   - What sound does the letter make?

5. Cut out the brand names, if possible, and paste them into the student's picture dictionary. Ask the student to dictate a sentence for each brand name (E.g., My kid loves to eat M&M's). Write the sentence in the student's dictionary.

Phonemic Awareness: Beginning Sounds
A Structured Approach

PURPOSE:

To build awareness of consonant sounds in the initial position of words.

STEPS:

1. Choose a sound that the student needs to learn (E.g., /s/).

2. Point to a picture of an object that begins with the sound /s/. Say, "This is soup. Listen to the word: soup. The word soup begins with the sound /s/." Point to other objects that begin with the sound /s/. Say the words one at a time and ask the student to repeat the word. (Flyers work well for this activity.)

3. Hold up a card with the letter "s" on it. Say, "This is the letter 's.' The sound /s/ goes with the letter 's.'"

4. Name a few objects in the room (E.g., scissors, clock, sock, pen, seat, book) and hold up the card every time the word begins with /s/.

5. Give the "s" card to the student. Say several words and ask the student to hold up the "s" card when they hear the sound /s/ at the beginning of the word.

6. Teach the student to print the letter "s." Ask the student to list the numbers from one to ten on a piece of paper. Read a list of ten words. Ask the student to print an "s" next to the number of the words that begin with the sound /s/.

Notes:

Continuous consonant sounds such as /s/, /m/, and /f/ should be the first sounds you use to teach phonemic awareness.

Adult students do not need to learn all the phonemes; they just need to demonstrate awareness that spoken words are made up of sounds.

These steps can also be used to build awareness of consonant sounds in the final position of words.

The sound /s/ is easier to hear when it is followed by a vowel (E.g., soup and sausage as opposed to stew and spinach).

Phonemic Awareness: Beginning Sounds
A Holistic Approach

DIALOGUE	TEXT	COMMENTS
Educator: We've read this story several times. This time, I want you to think about the sounds in the story. I'll read the first sentence and I want you to listen for /s/ words.		Select a familiar piece of text that you have read together several times. If the student does not understand the term "sentence," use another word or phrase such as "line" or "part of the story."
Student: Okay		
Educator: Tell me when you hear a word that begins with /s/.	Soccer is the game that I like better than any other game.	
Student: I heard an /s/ word. I can't remember what it was.		
Educator: That's okay. Let's try again. This time you can say the word as soon as you hear it.	Soccer is the…	The educator provides one way to reduce memory load. You could also ask the student to make a signal when they hear the sound.
Student: Soccer!		
Educator: Good, you heard it. Soccer begins with /s/. I'll read the next sentence.	It seems like the people in North America don't play.	
Student: Seems?		
Educator: Yes, you're right. But you don't seem sure.		The educator observes the student's hesitant response.
Student: Well, seems starts with /s/. But it's like I hear another one.		
Educator: Good listening. Seems starts with /s/ and ends with /s/.		After this activity, you could ask the student to circle the words in the text that start with "s."

Teaching Beginning Readers

Phonemic Awareness: Sound Boxes

PURPOSE:

To hear sounds in words and to make connections between letters and sounds.

STEPS:

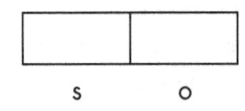

① Prepare cards on which blank squares are drawn for each sound unit in words.

② Choose a consonant-vowel (CV) word such as "so," "my," or "go."

③ Have the students blend sounds to make a word. Say, "I'm going to say the sounds for a word: /sss/ pause /ooo/. What is the word?" (Stretch out the sounds and pause between the sounds.) If the student cannot blend the letters to produce the target word, provide them with the word.

④ Have the student say the word slowly.

⑤ Repeat the word slowly and move a marker, such as a coin, into a box as each sound is pronounced (E.g., Say, /sss/ and push a coin into the first box).

⑥ Repeat steps 2, 3, and 4 with another CV word. Then ask the student to say the word slowly and move a coin into a box as they pronounce each sound.

Notes: As an alternative, you can have the student tap out the sounds they hear. Or, the student can make a fist and raise a finger for each sound they hear.

You can also have the student segment the word into sounds (E.g., Say the word "me" and have the student say the two different sounds /m/ and /e/).

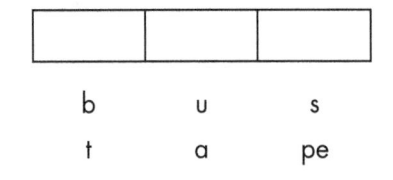

After the student has mastered CV words, you can introduce CVC words such as "bus" or "job." Then progress to CVCV words such as "tape" and "like."

Once the student can hear sounds in words, apply this activity to spelling. Replace the markers with letter tiles from a scrabble game. Ask, "What sound do you hear? Which letter makes the sound? Where will you put the letter?" Or, have the student print the letter or letters representing the sound in each box.

44 Print-Sound Relationship Strategies

Phonics

PURPOSE:

To teach the relationships between letters and sounds.

STEPS:

1. Present the student with a sight word that begins with a consonant or consonant blend they need to learn (E.g., soup).

2. Point to the letter "s" in "soup." Say, "Soup starts with the letter 's.' The sound that goes with the letter 's' is /s/. Say /s/."

3. Introduce other words that begin with the sound /s/. Say, "These words also begin with the sound /s/: sand, seal, soft. Can you think of some other words that begin with the sound /s/?"

4. Prepare a list of ten words. At least five of the words should begin with the sound /s/. Say, "I'm going to say ten words. Listen carefully to each word. If the word begins with the sound /s/, nod your head or say 'yes.'" Say the ten words to the student.

5. Read a short news article to the student. Discuss the article. Then ask the student to circle the words in the text that begin with the letter "s."

6. At the next lesson, repeat steps 1 to 5, but modify the activities so that the student works with words that end with the sound /s/.

Note:

If the student finds it difficult to remember a letter-sound relationship, ask them to choose a key word (E.g., sun for "s").

Word Families

PURPOSE:

To recognize familiar patterns in unfamiliar words.

STEPS:

1. Choose a word that the student can read from a language experience story or their word bank. The word needs to contain a common letter pattern (E.g., back).

2. Ask the student to read the word and then pronounce the sound of the first letter. Then ask the student to pronounce the next chunk of letters (E.g., /back/; /b/ /ack/).

3. Print the letter pattern at the top of a blank sheet of paper. List two words that belong to the word family below the printed letter pattern.

ack
back
rack

4. Read the two words and ask, "What do you notice about these words?"

5. Have the student generate more words that have the same pattern. Ask, "Can you think of more words that look and sound the same?" Add the student's words to the list.

6. Have the student read each word on the list by sounding out the first consonant and then the letter pattern (E.g., b / ack/; back). Explain that reading becomes easier when the student can identify and sound out chunks of letters in words.

A word family consists of words that rhyme and contain the same letter pattern.

Notes:

Students need to know consonant sounds and how to rhyme in order to experience success with word families.

A word slide can be used to practise word families (See page 57).

Most Common Letter Patterns

–ack	–ay	–ip
–ail	–eat	–it
–ain	–ell	–ock
–ake	–est	–oke
–ale	–ice	–op
–ame	–ide	–ore
–an	–ick	–ot
–ank	–ight	–uck
–ap	–ill	–ug
–ash	–in	–ump
–at	–ine	–unk
–ate	–ing	
–aw	–ink	

Source: Cunningham, P. M. (2009). *Phonics they use: Words for reading and writing* (5th ed.). Toronto, ON: Pearson.

WRITING

Frame Sentences

PURPOSE:

To experience success in writing sentences.

STEPS:

1. Select a topic with the student.

2. Make an idea map. Print the topic in the centre.

3. Brainstorm words and ideas about the topic. Add them to the map.

4. Create a set of frame sentences that can be completed with the brainstormed words.

5. Ask the student to complete the frame sentences, using the map as a reference.

Possible Topics:

My job	Things I like to eat
My neighbour	Things I like to do
My best friend	Things I like to cook
Favourite smells	Fears
Favourite shows	Beliefs
Riding the bus	Wishes

48 Writing Strategies

```
           happy
  smart     |    tough
       \    |    /
        ( grandson )
       /    |    \
  daring    |    cheeky
           strong
```

> My Grandson
>
> My grandson is smart.
>
> My grandson is tough.
>
> My grandson is a daredevil.
>
> My grandson is strong.
>
> My grandson is cheeky.
>
> My grandson is happy.

Emergent Writing

PURPOSE:

To build awareness that letters in written words represent sounds in spoken words.

DIALOGUE	STUDENT WRITING	COMMENTS
Educator: Would you like to try writing a few words?		
Student: I can't write.		
Educator: Lots of adults find it hard to write. We'll just practise.		It is important for the student to know that many people find it difficult to write.
Student: What would I write?		
Educator: How about a grocery list? I want you to think of something you buy at the grocery store.		You can also give the student the option to write whatever they want.
Student: Buns?		
Educator: Okay, let's stretch out the word like this: /ccc/ooo/fff/eee. How many sounds do you hear?		
Student: Three?		Many students will not hear the sound /o/ in coffee.
Educator: Now, listen to the sound at the beginning of "coffee," and write the letter that goes with that sound.		
Student: Like this?	k	It does not matter if the word is misspelled. The point is to foster awareness that letters represent sounds.
Educator: Good. One sound, one letter. Now, write down the other sounds you hear in coffee.		
Student: cccofffeee. coffee.	kfe	Invite the student to carry out a similar process, stretching words out and writing letters for the sounds they are able to hear.

50 Writing Strategies

Look, Say, Cover, Print, and Check

PURPOSE:

To use visual memory to spell words.

STEPS:

1. Print five words the student wants to learn in the New Words column. The student **looks** at the word and thinks about how they will remember it.

2. The student **says** the word out loud. The student closes their eyes and tries to see the whole word.

3. The student **covers** the word with their hand or a piece of paper.

4. The student **prints** the word in the Day 1 column and says the word while printing it.

5. The student **checks** the word, letter by letter, to see if they have spelled it correctly. The student circles or highlights any parts that are misspelled. Print the correct spelling below the word.

   During the week, repeat the process two more times. Use the columns for Day 2 and Day 3.

NEW WORDS	DAY 1	DAY 2	DAY 3
milk	mik milk		
eggs	eggs		
bread	berd bread		
cheese	chez cheese		
bacon	bekon bacon		

Teaching Beginning Readers 51

ACTIVITIES

Photo Album

PURPOSES:

To provide the student with familiar, meaningful text that is predictable and easy to read.

To establish the link between spoken and written words.

STEPS:

1. Purchase a photo album at the dollar store. Have the student bring in some photos that document a specific event, trip, person, animal, etc. (E.g., ice-fishing photos).

2. Have the student provide a caption for the first photo. Ask, "What is happening in this photo?" Record the caption, making sure the student can see the words being printed. Record the student's exact words, printing clearly. Say each word as you print it.

3. Read the caption, pointing to each word as you read.

4. Read the caption together, tracking the words with your finger. Have the student read the caption independently. If the student falters, provide support by reading the word.

5. Repeat steps 2 to 4 for each photo. Reread the captions at the next lesson.

Note:

Classroom educators could build this activity into their daily routine.

My Grandkids

Jeremy goes for a ride on his slide.

Jeremy tries out his fishing rod.

Maia holds a butterfly.

Maia pats a pony.

Sight Word Bingo

PURPOSE:

To practise sight words.

STEPS:

1. Make a bingo card with three squares across and three squares down. Print the word FREE in the middle square. Photocopy a card for each student in the group or class.

2. List twelve sight words the students want to learn. Print eight of the words in the squares on the bingo cards, making sure that you print different words on each bingo card.

3. Give each student a bingo card and markers. Instruct the students to cover their words with the markers as they hear the words read out loud and to call out "Bingo" when they have covered all the words on their bingo card.

4. Read the words from the list of 12 sight words, in random order. The first student to call "Bingo" can be the caller for the next game. (You might need to help the caller read some of the words.)

Notes:

You can also play sight word Bingo using the words from a specific word family (E.g., pay, fay, gay, lay, may, bay, hay, day).

On your computer, search "bingo card maker" or "bingo card generator." You will find free programs that allow you to create sets of bingo cards.

Photo Stories

PURPOSES:

To stimulate discussion on a common social issue.

To create a language experience story with a group, supported by photos.

STEPS:

1. Work together with the students to identify an issue, concern, or dilemma. The issue of shelter, for example, might include a discussion of landlords, tenants' rights, crowded living conditions, or safety.

2. Invite the students to share their experiences. Facilitate a discussion about their experiences.

3. Discuss an outline for the students' photo story.

4. Tape lined flip-chart paper on the walls around the classroom. Facilitate a process that enables the students to dictate the story by asking simple questions such as "What would you like to say on this page? Do you want to add anything else?"

5. Record the students' exact words, printing clearly on every second line of the flip-chart paper. Say each word as you print it. Ask the students if they want to make any changes.

6. Facilitate a discussion of the photo that will accompany each page of text. Sketch the accompanying photo below the text on each sheet of flip-chart paper. Make a list of props that are needed for each photo. Find volunteers to take the photos.

7. Create the photo story by typing up the text on sheets of paper and inserting the accompanying photographs. Bind the sheets into a booklet.

Note:

For the students' first photo story, you could introduce a topic of interest rather than a social issue. This would give students time to gain the skills of visual storytelling. For example, you could facilitate a discussion about places of interest in the community.

Picture Dictionary

PURPOSE:

To create a personal dictionary to use as a reference for reading and spelling.

STEPS:

1. Explain how and why a dictionary is used. Point out that a dictionary is organized alphabetically.

2. Tell the student that they can use the words in a personal dictionary to help them spell. Provide the student with a notebook. Head each page with an upper and lower case letter (E.g., Aa). Allow at least two pages per letter.

3. Bring in some flyers and magazines. Ask the student to cut out pictures that represent words they want to know how to spell. For example, a student might cut out pictures of food items they might include on a shopping list, such as coffee, bread, and juice.

4. Have the student paste the picture under the appropriate letter in the dictionary. Print the name of the item on a piece of paper. Have the student copy the word next to the picture of the item.

Word Slide

PURPOSE:

To build words using common letter patterns.

STEPS:

1. Choose a word family with a common letter pattern (E.g., *ay*).

2. Cut two strips from an 8½ x 11-inch piece of paper.

    Strip A is 8½ x 1½ inches; strip B is 9 x 3½ inches.

3. Fold strip A in half. Cut a window in strip A. Glue or tape the side edge of strip A together. Print the letter pattern to the right of the window. Print the first one or two letters of the word family down the centre of strip B.

4. Slowly pull strip B through strip A. Ask the student to read the words as the letters on strip B line up with the printed word pattern on strip A.

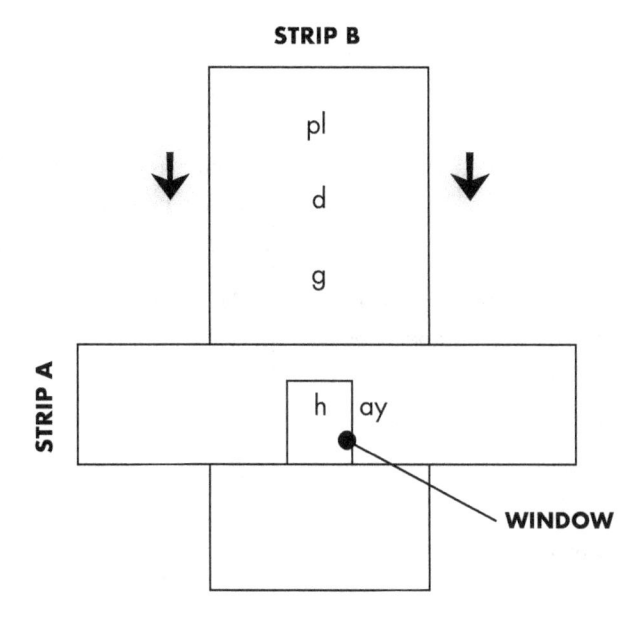

ay
bay
day
gay
gray
hay
jay
lay
may
pay
play
pray
ray
say
stay
tray
way

STRIP B

pl

d

g

STRIP A

h | ay

— **WINDOW**

Note:

Word slides can also be used to expose words rapidly for sight word recognition practice.

Teaching Beginning Readers **57**

LESSON PLAN

Guidelines for Successful Learning

GUIDELINE	WHY	HOW
Create a safe environment.	Students will be more willing to take risks, speak their mind, and engage in critical thinking.	Praise risk-taking. View errors as a learning opportunity. Take time to discuss students' concerns and challenges.
Use effective communication skills.	Students find it difficult to answer questions that are unclear or to respond to complicated and/or ambiguous directions.	Be an active listener. Allow time for students to ask and answer questions. Give clear explanations.
Move from the familiar to the unfamiliar and from simple to more complex tasks.	Students are more apt to experience success if they can use the extensive knowledge they bring to the instructional context.	Use what students already know as a starting point for each lesson.
Incorporate activity-oriented learning.	Field trips provide opportunities for students to engage in literacy practices outside of school.	Take trips to the library, the grocery store, etc. Visit a community project or listen to a community speaker.
Build time for review into every lesson.	You need to ensure that students have learned and retained new concepts and skills.	Ask students to explain or demonstrate what they have learned.
Monitor progress and evaluate lessons.	Students will learn and make progress when instruction is continually tailored to their needs.	Observe students' verbal and non-verbal responses to activities. Ask students to describe what they liked and disliked about the lesson. Ask students which activities were easy and which were hard, and why.

Case Study: Troy's Story

Troy is married, with two children. For the past ten years, he has worked as a plumber. Troy relies on his wife to help him complete work orders. Troy works long days, usually 12 to 14 hours, and has little leisure time to pursue hobbies. To relax, Troy enjoys watching sports on TV.

Troy was born in Newfoundland and attended school up to Grade 7. He enjoyed math and phys.ed., but found reading difficult. Troy managed to pass tests by guessing the answers.

Troy just turned 40. He wants to get certified as a plumber so that he will be entitled to the union's wage rates. However, as a beginning reader, Troy is not able to complete the course work required for certification. Troy's co-workers have no idea that Troy has problems with reading and writing. They cannot understand why he hasn't obtained his certification papers.

Troy is a fast learner. He has a strong auditory memory, which allows him to remember detailed verbal instructions. However, work is becoming increasingly difficult as technology creeps into the workplace. Troy has learned how to use a GPS but is stumped by addresses that require him to read names rather than numbers. Troy cannot write, yet his boss wants him to use email and text messaging as a primary form of communication. As well, Troy is being required to complete more paperwork. He has to document his customers' methods of payment, but he can't spell American Express and MasterCard.

Troy's Assessment

Troy's assessment indicated that he has a strong visual memory, as he recognized many sight words. These sight words included environmental print and high-frequency words. He knows all the letter names and the sounds that go with consonants, but Troy does not know the vowel sounds.

Troy's Lesson Plan
Week 1

ACTIVITY	MATERIALS	TEACHING STRATEGY
Objectives: To provide familiar, meaningful text that is predictable and easy to read. To establish the link between spoken and written words. **Time:** 15 minutes		
Talk to Troy about common plumbing jobs (E.g., fixing a leaky tap). Write a short language experience story about a common plumbing job. Read the story several times together and then have Troy read it independently. If Troy can't read a word, ask him to predict a word that makes sense.	pen, paper	Language Experience (See page 22.)
Objective: To increase repertoire of sight words. **Time:** 30 minutes (Take a short break sometime during this activity.)		
Explain the importance of sight words. Ask Troy to circle 3 to 5 words in his language experience story that he can use when he writes emails and text messages. Follow the steps for making a personal dictionary.	notebook for personal dictionary flyers that contain pictures of common bathroom fixtures and plumbing tools scissors, paste or tape	Sight words (See page 26.) Personal Dictionary (See page 56.)
Objective: To look for familiar patterns in unfamiliar words. **Time:** 15 minutes		
Choose a word from Troy's story that contains a common letter pattern (E.g., tap). Follow the steps for teaching a word family.	language experience story	Word Families (See page 46.)
Objective: To engage in active reading. **Time:** 15 minutes		
Read *Tony's Deal*, which is a photo story about a plumber. Follow the steps for Directed Reading Thinking Activity.	*Tony's Deal*	Directed Reading Thinking Activity (See page 32.)

60 Lesson Planning

Troy's Lesson Plan
Week 2

ACTIVITY	MATERIALS	TEACHING STRATEGY
Objective: To increase reading fluency. **Time:** 15 minutes		
Read *Tony's Deal*, following the steps for the echo reading strategy. Discuss the ethical dilemma in the story.	*Tony's Deal*	Echo Reading (See page 37.)
Objective: To increase repertoire of sight words. **Time:** 25 minutes		
Ask Troy to add more words to his personal dictionary. Meanwhile, print sight words learned in Week 1 on index cards. Ask Troy to read them. Have Troy choose three words that he wants to learn to spell. Demonstrate the Look, Say, Cover, Print, and Check strategy.	personal dictionary index cards paper	Sight Words (See page 26.) Look, Say, Cover, Print, and Check (See page 51.)
Objective: To look for familiar patterns in unfamiliar words. **Time:** 10 minutes		
Review word family from Week 1, using a word slide. Choose another common letter pattern to learn from Troy's sight words.	word slide	Word Slide (See page 57.) Word Families (See page 46.)
Objective: To increase fluency. **Time:** 5 to 10 minutes		
Explain the Repeated Reading strategy. Ask Troy to choose either his language experience story or *Tony's Deal*. Time Troy's reading, and record.	*Tony's Deal* language experience story	Repeated Reading (See page 38.)

Future Lessons:
(1) Introduce frame sentences. Choose a common frame that Troy might use in a text message or email.
(2) Introduce short vowel sounds. Use a phonemic awareness activity such as the sound boxes.

Teaching Beginning Readers

Lesson Plan Form

ACTIVITY	RESOURCES	TEACHING STRATEGY
Objective: **Time:**		
Objective: **Time:**		
Objective: **Time:**		
Objective: **Time:**		

Case Study: Pitseolak's Story

Pitseolak's parents were born in Manitoba. They did not place a high value on education because of their negative experiences in residential school. Their residential school experience resulted in a fractured first language because they were not allowed to speak Inuktitut. Consequently, Pitseolak did not attend school on a regular basis and didn't develop effective language skills as a child. When Pitseolak did attend, her language skills interfered with her ability to learn. She began to use drugs, making it difficult to concentrate at school. Pitseolak dropped out of school when she was 14, after having a child.

Pitseolak now lives in an isolated Arctic community located on Baffin Island in the Canadian territory of Nunavut. She is single, with three sons, one daughter, and three grandchildren. She is currently unemployed. In the past, she has worked as a daycare support worker and as a custodian. She also volunteers with the community's breakfast program and Christmas committee. Pitseolak likes to listen to music, and with her daughter's help, is able to download music from the Internet. She enjoys doing beadwork on leather purses.

Pitseolak loves being a grandmother and wants to read to her grandchildren. She also wants to learn how to read non-fiction stories, particularly ones relating to Inuit culture and Nunavut.

Pitseolak's Assessment

Pitseolak lacks confidence in her ability to learn. Pitseolak speaks both English and Inuktitut well enough to interact socially. She did not learn to read Inuktitut, but she knows a few English sight words and the letter names. Her phonics knowledge and phonemic awareness is quite limited.

Pitseolak's Lesson Plan
Week 1

ACTIVITY	MATERIALS	TEACHING STRATEGY
Objectives: To provide familiar, meaningful text that is predictable and easy to read. To establish the link between spoken and written words. **Time:** 30 minutes		
Arrange the photos and put into a photo album. Ask Pitseolak to describe who is in the first photo and what is happening. Write a caption for the photo. Read the caption together several times. Then ask Pitseolak to read it independently. Repeat this strategy for a few more photos.	photos of student's grandchildren photo album	Language Experience (See page 22.)
Objective: To increase repertoire of sight words. **Time:** 15 minutes		
Explain the importance of sight words. Ask Pitseolak to look at the sentences in the photo album. Ask her to point to her grandchildren's names. Have her copy each name onto a separate index card. Ask Pitseolak to point to two other words she would like to learn. Have her copy them on index cards.	index cards pens	Sight Words (See page 26.)
Objective: To increase fluency. **Time:** 15 minutes		
Bring in some easy-to-read children's books about Inuit culture or Nunavut. Ask Pitseolak to choose a book. Explain that you will read it together during the lesson, and that eventually she will be able to read it to her grandchildren.	library books	Echo Reading (See page 37.)
Objective: To build awareness of consonant sounds in the initial position of words. **Time:** 15 minutes		
Introduce the /s/ sound. Explain that you are going to do some work with sounds.	pictures of objects language experience story	Phonemic Awareness (See page 42.)

Pitseolak's Lesson Plan
Week 2

ACTIVITY	MATERIALS	TEACHING STRATEGY
Objective: To develop fluency. **Time:** 30 minutes		
Ask Pitseolak to read the captions in her photo album. Talk about and add captions to more photos.	photo album index cards	Repeated Reading (p. 38) Language Experience (See page 22.)
Objective: To copy words from index cards to a calendar. **Time:** 10 minutes		
Review the sight words Pitseolak learned last week. Introduce the calendar. Ask Pitseolak to fill the calendar with her grandchildren's birthdays. She can refer to her index cards to spell the names.	calendar	Sight Words (See page 26.)
Objective: To develop fluency. **Time:** 15 minutes		
Continue reading the children's book.	children's book	Echo Reading (p. 37)
Objective: To increase repertoire of sight words. **Time:** 15 minutes		
Ask Pitseolak to choose some five more sight words.	photo album children's books	Sight Words (See page 26.)
Objective: To build awareness of consonant sounds in the initial position of words. **Time:** 10 minutes		
Continue working with the sound /s/, using the first sentence of the children's book. Then, introduce the sound /m/.	children's book	Phonemic Awareness
Objective: To find a song, using the Internet **Time:** 10 minutes		
Choose an Inuit singer such as Susan Aglukark. Help Pitseolak download one of her songs.	Internet	

Future Lessons:
(1) Transcribe the lyrics to the song and bring them to the next lesson. Read the song, using echo reading.
(2) Continue to develop Pitseolak's phonemic awareness and gradually introduce phonics.

Teaching Beginning Readers **65**

English as a Second Language Group

Patsy teaches a group of ESL students one evening a week. Patsy works with Rod, a volunteer. The class, which runs for two and a half hours, includes a 20-minute break. The students can communicate basic ideas in English. The students received little education in their home country and never learned to read or write in their own language. Some of the students have developed some basic literacy skills such as the understanding that print conveys meaning and phonemic awareness.

During the first hour, the group works together on reading, speaking, and listening activities. Patsy facilitates conversation and role-playing activities on topics of interest to promote communication skills. Every month, the group explores one theme such as health care, the workplace, or shelter. Small group activities include the development of photostories and language experience stories, as well as echo reading.

After a 20-minute break, the group reconvenes into pairs made up of students with similar strengths and weaknesses. Patsy has developed three learning stations. In Station 1, a student pair works on one computer. In Station 2, students work independently with some assistance from Rod. In Station 3, Patsy provides a mini-lesson to two students. Rod's role is to assist students at Stations 1 and 2. For instance, the students always need help with starting the software program.

CLASS ACTIVITIES	Discuss landlord and tenants' rights. Improvise a role-play about a landlord and tenant. Develop a photostory.		
STUDENT PAIRS	**Station 1** **Computer**	**Station 2** **Independent**	**Station 3** **Mini-Lesson**
Jamal **Dahia**	*Kurzweil 3000* (reading support software)	Picture Dictionary (See page 56.) Practise printing skills by copying a story.	Repeated Reading (See page 38.) Phonics (See page 45.)
Maria **Franko**	*You Be the Judge* (read-along CD)	Picture Dictionary (See page 56.) Practise printing skills by copying a story.	Repeated Reading (See page 38.) Phonemic Awareness (See page 42.)
Chara **Rosa**	*The Alphabet* (software)	Listen to taped books	Use a language experience story to teach print concepts and conventions.

Values and Beliefs
Reflection Activity

Our values and beliefs affect the way we work with students and approach instruction. Make two photocopies of this page and respond to the following questions. In six months, answer the questions again. Compare your answers to see if your values and beliefs have changed.

Date: _____

What are your values and beliefs with respect to teaching and learning?

_____
_____
_____
_____
_____
_____
_____

Where and how did you learn your values and beliefs? How do these beliefs affect your instruction?

_____
_____
_____
_____
_____
_____
_____

Resources

DICTIONARIES

PUBLISHER: OXFORD
TITLE: THE OXFORD PICTURE DICTIONARY

This illustrated, theme-based dictionary presents 4,000 words and phrases within meaningful, real-life contexts. The themes, which include food, clothing, health, housing, community, transportation, and work, meet the needs of beginning and low-intermediate level students. On each page, vibrant, full-colour illustrations portray the words. Each unit closes with an illustrated story that presents vocabulary in context and is followed by discussion questions.

PHOTO STORIES

PUBLISHER: GRASS ROOTS PRESS
TITLE: GRASS ROOTS READERS

Emergent readers will appreciate the relevant content and readability of these photo stories. Each page includes a captivating photograph and one or two short sentences. The photographs reflect the text, making the words easier to decode.

The 24 titles are organized under six themes: Health, Humour, Animals, How To, You Be the Judge, and Romance. These compelling photo stories are guaranteed to provide beginning readers with a positive reading experience.

EASY READERS AND TAPED BOOKS

PUBLISHER: NEWLEAF BOOKS, ENGLAND
TITLE: BEGINNER READERS

The books provide an uncluttered format. Each page has large print and a clear layout. High-grade paper is used so there is no show-through to distract a beginner reader.

The language is familiar and the books are beautifully illustrated to support new readers with a set of visual clues to the text. Audio CDs are available to accompany all of the Beginner Reader books. students can enjoy listening to the story as it is read. There is also a slower reading on Track 2 to help adult learners read the words in the book.

PUBLISHER: PRACE, AUSTRALIA
TITLE: PAGE TURNERS LEVEL 1 BOOKS

Beginning readers will enjoy these entertaining, engaging, and easy-to-read stories. Each story is illustrated with amusing line drawings. The books were produced by teachers to meet the needs of their students.

PUBLISHER: GRASS ROOTS PRESS
TITLES: BE THE JUDGE SERIES
ROMANCE SERIES

Each series contains four photo stories and a read-along CD, which allows students to read the stories independently. Audio is provided for entire sentences and/or individual words. On each screen, the student is provided with a full-colour photograph and one or two lines of predictable text.

PUBLISHER: AXIS EDUCATION
TITLE: THIS LIFE READERS

This series of ten fresh, quirky stories is great fun to read. The 32-page stories contain one or two short, simple sentences per page printed in a clear font,-and plenty of repetition and reinforcement. These high-interest readers nurture student confidence, help keep students motivated, and build a bridge between reading to learn and reading for pleasure. The series includes a resource package of literacy activities that can be photocopied.

SOFTWARE

PUBLISHER: PROTEA TEXTWARE LTD.
TITLE: THE ALPHABET

This highly interactive, self-paced program facilitates the learning of the alphabet through several activities. Students will receive instruction and practice in the following areas:
- sight-sound relationships
- upper- and lower-case matching
- alphabetical order
- copying and spelling words
- keyboarding skills

PUBLISHER: KURZWEIL EDUCATIONAL SYSTEMS
TITLE: KURZWEIL 3000

Kurzweil 3000 is able to read aloud virtually any electronic file on a computer or on the Internet, using synthetic speech. The software reads text aloud at a rate appropriate to each user, providing a model of and support for fluent reading.

PUBLISHER: ODIOGO
TITLE: TEXT READING SOFTWARE

Odiogo transforms news sites and blog posts into high fidelity, near-human quality audio files that are ready to download and play anywhere, anytime, on any device. The Odiogo generated content can be listened to on Windows/Mac PCs, mobile phones, and iPods/MP3 players.

Glossary

ALPHABETIC PRINCIPLE

The understanding that letters in written words stand for sounds in spoken words. Individuals demonstrate this understanding when they are able to map letters onto sounds to spell words or map sounds onto letters to identify words.

AUTHENTIC TEXT

Print materials that represent the real world (E.g., bus schedules, cereal boxes, bank statements, flyers).

CLOZE PROCEDURE

An instructional strategy that encourages students to use meaning and grammar cues to restore deleted words from a piece of text.

DIRECTED READING THINKING ACTIVITY (DRTA)

A step-by-step instructional activity that encourages readers to use their background knowledge to predict what might happen in a story and to use cues from the text to evaluate and revise these predictions.

ECHO READING

An activity in which the educator reads through a text, sentence by sentence, tracking each word with their finger. The student echos the educator by reading each sentence independently.

ENVIRONMENTAL PRINT

Print and graphic symbols found in the physical environments of the home, community, and workplace (E.g., street signs, food product labels, logos).

FLUENCY

The ability to read in a smooth, expressive, and accurate manner at an appropriate rate and with good comprehension.

HIGH-FREQUENCY WORDS

The most common words in our written language.

INFERENCE

A conclusion drawn from combining a person's background knowledge with information from the text.

INSTRUCTIONAL READING LEVEL

The level at which a student reads with adequate comprehension and word recognition. A student who is reading at their instructional level has more than adequate comprehension (70 to 90 percent) and a high level of word recognition (91 to 98 percent) but would still benefit from some instruction in these areas.

K-W-L

A framework that elicits a student's background knowledge and level of interest prior to their reading expository text, in order to establish a purpose for reading and help readers reflect upon their reading.

LANGUAGE EXPERIENCE

An integrated writing-reading-discussion activity in which the instructor records a dictated story or personal anecdote from a student or group of students. Language experience stories provide the student with familiar and meaningful text that is highly predictable and easy to read.

PHONEME

The smallest unit of sound that changes the meaning of spoken words. English has about 41 to 44 phonemes. The word "read," for example, contains three phonemes: /r/, /ea/, and /d/.

PHONEMIC AWARENESS

The ability to hear, identify, and work with the individual sounds, or phonemes, in spoken words.

PHONICS KNOWLEDGE

Involves an understanding of the alphabetic principle and the relationship between the letters of written language and their spoken sounds.

SIGHT WORDS

The words a student can read and pronounce accurately and automatically.

THINK-ALOUD STRATEGY

A strategy that utilizes the modelling process. The educator verbalizes their own thoughts while reading a passage orally so that students will realize how readers interact with text.

WORD FAMILY

A group of words that rhyme and contain the same letter pattern (E.g., beam, dream, seam, team, steam, scream).

References

Campbell, P. (2010). *Diagnostic adult reading assessment for beginning readers*. (DALA). Edmonton, AB: Grass Roots Press.

Campbell, P. (2003). *Teaching reading to adults: A balanced approach*. Edmonton, AB: Grass Roots Press.

Campbell, P., & Malicky, G. (2002). The reading strategies of adult basic education students. *Adult Basic Education, 12*(1), 3-19.

Carmel, B.A. (2003). *Understanding the roots of illiteracy: Adult beginning readers' explanations of why they did not learn to read*. (Unpublished doctoral dissertation). New York University, New York, NY.

Center for Educational Research and Innovation [CERI]. (2005). *Formative assessment: Improving learning in secondary classrooms*. Paris, France: OECD.

Centre for Family Literacy. (2006). *Literacy tutor's guide*. Edmonton, AB: Author.

Clay, M. M. (2002). *An observation survey of early literacy achievement* (2nd ed.). Portsmouth, NH: Heinemann.

Cunningham, P. M. (2009). *Phonics they use: Words for reading and writing* (5th ed.). Toronto, ON: Pearson.

Ewing, G. (1994). *Don't talk to me about vowels*. Toronto, ON: Metro Toronto Movement for Literacy.

Hunt, J. (2005). *Learning tools that work: A survey of adaptive technology in learning programs*. Action Read: Guelph, ON. Available from http://www.nald.ca/library/learning/lttw/lttw.pdf

Jacobson, E., Degener, S., & Purcell-Gates, V. (2003). *Creating authentic materials and activities for the adult literacy classroom: A handbook for practitioners*. Boston, MA: NCSALL. Retrieved from http://www.ncsall.net/fileadmin/resources/teach/jacobson.pdf

MacGregor, R. (2006, October 7). 100 years old and a man of letters; After 93 years of living, Clarence Brazier began the fight of his life—to learn to read. *The Globe and Mail*.

Ouchi, M. (2005). In S. Rogers (Ed.), *Book lovers*. Edmonton, AB: Grass Roots Press.

Prior, J., & Gerard, M. R. (2004). *Environmental print in the classroom: Meaningful connections for learning to read*. Newark, DE: International Reading Association.

Purcell-Gates, V. (1996). Stories, coupons, and the TV guide: Relationships between home literacy experiences and emergent literacy knowledge. *Reading Research Quarterly*, 31(4), 406-428.

Purcell-Gates, V., Jacobson, E., & Degener, S. (2004). *Print literacy development: Uniting the cognitive and social practice theories*. Cambridge, MA: Harvard University Press.

CPSIA information can be obtained
at www.ICGtesting.com
Printed in the USA
LVHW101235180521
687666LV00031B/948

9 781926 583136